The Permanent Floating Voluntary Society

By: Kerry Thornley
LIBERTY UNDER ATTACK PUBLICATIONS

Copyleft Notice

This book is covered by a BipCot NoGovernment License. Re-use and modification is permitted to anyone EXCEPT for governments and the bludgies thereof.

Further Use Permission: Please feel free to use, re-use, distribute, copy, re-print, take credit for, steal, broadcast, mock, hate, quote, misquote, or modify this book in any way you see fit. Sell it, make copies and hand it out at concerts, make t-shirts, print it on flying disks, or do anything else because intellectual property is a State based haven of the weak, the stupid, and those lacking confidence in their own ability.

Disclaimer

The purpose of this short book is to provide individuals with possible solutions for finding freedom on the open ocean. Many of these solutions are perfectly legal, some are in a gray area, but some are outright illegal. That said, neither the author nor the publisher recommend or advocate anyone break the law. If you decide to pursue any solutions presented in this book, it is done at your own risk and of your own accord. In other words, be smart and practice excellent security culture.

Looking for your next read or listen?

Looking for your next read or listen?

1. **Adventures in Illinois Law: Witnessing Tyranny Firsthand** by Shane Radliff (Audiobook/Anthology)
2. **Adventures in Illinois Higher Education: Communist Indoctrination** by Shane Radliff (Audiobook/Anthology)
3. **An Illusive Phantom of Hope: A Critique of Reformism** by Kyle Rearden (Audiobook/Anthology)
4. **The Production of Security** by Gustave de Molinari (Audiobook)
5. **Are Cops Constitutional?** by Roger Roots (Audiobook)
6. **Vonu: The Search for Personal Freedom** by Rayo (Audiobook)
7. **Argumentation Ethics: An Anthology** by Hans-Herman Hoppe et al (Anthology)
8. **Just Below The Surface: A Guide to Security Culture** by Kyle Rearden (Audiobook/Anthology)
9. **Sedition, Subversion, and Sabotage, Field Manual No. 1: A Three Part Solution to the State** by Ben Stone (Audiobook)
10. **#agora** by anonymous (Paperback and Kindle)
11. **Vonu: A Strategy for Self-Liberation** by Shane Radliff (Paperback/Audiobook)
12. **Second Realm: Book on Strategy** by Smuggler and XYZ (Paperback)
13. **Vonu: The Search for Personal Freedom** by Rayo (Special Paperback Reprint/Audiobook)
14. **Vonu: The Search for Personal Freedom, Part 2 [Letters From Rayo]** (Paperback)
15. **Going Mobile** by Tom Marshall (Paperback/Audiobook)
16. **Anarchist to Abolitionist: A Bad Quaker's Journey** by Ben Stone
17. **Brushfire, A Thriller** by Matthew Wojtecki

VIEW THEM ALL AT LibertyUnderAttack.com!

Table of Contents

Transcriber's Foreword

Chapter I: Small Boats
Chapter II: Large Boats
Chapter III: Ships and Shipping
Chapter IV: Marine Cities
Chapter V: Aquaculture
Chapter VI: Marine Mining

Transcriber's Foreword

71% of Planet Earth is made up of wide open ocean. This translates into over **332,519,000** cubic miles of water, as estimated by the U.S. Geological Survey. And yet, in large part, humans have yet to even begin utilizing the seemingly endless possibilities abound.

Thankfully, the ocean has finally drawn the attention of libertarians in their efforts to be left the hell alone, investors seeking opportunities to profit, and entrepreneurs seeing the potential of medical research, aquaculture, architecture, and more, free from ridiculous, anti-innovative, primitive government regulations—great for them, and also great for you, the consumer.

Two notable projects have sprung up in this shift to the open ocean: *The Seasteading Institute* and *The Marinea Project* (TMP). TSI's goal is to build a seastead off the coast of their hosting nation state, French Polynesia, whereas TMP's is a village at sea in international waters, located near the Cay Sal Bank. Rather than coming up with brand new designs for expensive floating cities, TMP plans to utilize already existing (and proven) technology. Phase 1 consists of acquiring a "Floatel" (floating hotel) which would serve as the village, and individuals and families would live on their own boats.

But this idea is far from new. The publication you are about to read, *The Permanent Floating Voluntary Society*, is a collection of articles originally published in the libertarian publication, *Innovator*, from July to December 1966.

Herein, Kerry Thornley provides insight on getting started as a sailor, considerations for purchasing boats, potential shipping ventures, starting marine cities, aquaculture (ocean "farming"), and mining opportunities for entrepreneurs.

I hope these articles will inspire you to go against the grain and try something new, whether it's in pursuance of personal freedom, or just to expand your experiences as a human being.

In conclusion, I think Rayo, author of *Vonu: The Search for Personal Freedom*, put it best: "If your State of anchorage becomes intolerable, don't waste energy in extended public criticism or conflict; apply your free market principles by ***setting sail for sunnier waters***."

Shane Radliff
September 2017
The Vonu Podcast

Chapter 1: Small Boats

"What's the use of being a shipmaster if you can't tell people to go Hell?" – Old Captain's Proverb

The greater portion of this planet's surface is out of the effective control of any State, and yet libertarians complain that for the man who would be free there is "no place to go." This article is the first of a series dedicated to an exploration of the "ocean interstice" as a means to personal liberty and economic freedom.

SMALL BOATS

For as low as the price of a late-model car an individual can purchase a sea-worthy vessel large enough for a small family. This writer is acquainted with a couple who bought a used 26-feet yacht for somewhere around $500 and lived aboard, with their small daughter, sailing the Pacific for a year. Since these folks were not adverse to a steady diet of fresh sea food, expenses were quite low – for, as the man of the family pointed out, "There was no place to spend money out there." (And on a previous voyage to the Virgin Islands they had stocked up on rum at $1.25 a gallon.)

For the less adventurous a slightly larger investment will fill the galley with dry-land staples. And for those who want to get grim about investing money on a boat, it is no problem to spend over $30,000 for a fancy yacht. But suitable used – or brand new – boats can be had for much less.

You can save yourself time by first getting some book learning – particularly with regard to sailing terminology, a small language in itself very important for conversing with instructors and other sailors. After you learn the difference between a jib and jibe, and learn the origin of such colorful terms in everyday English as landfall, leeway, tack, bilge, and mainstay you are ready to take a course in theoretical sailing and/or small boat safety. Such courses are given gratis by the U.S. Power Squadrons, which comprise a national private organization dedicated to on-the-water safety. And for libertarians who don't mind sanctioning the State, both the U.S. Coast Guard and many public adult night schools offer similar instruction.

The next step is to go out on the water under the supervision of a competent sailor. The market rate for such practical lessons at this time in Southern California is around $10 an hour – including boat rental – and worth every penny of it. Six hours of such supervised sailing ought to make you about ready to go it alone – for gradually lengthening trial runs – during which you can teach yourself to navigate, with the help of any good advanced sailing manual.

By this time, if you have not been doing so before, you will probably be keeping an eye out for that special boat that fits YOU. A sailing vessel with a motor of some kind is probably the best bet for exploring the ocean "interstice" on a small scale – combining fuel economy with flexibility. There are boats made of steel, fiberglass, and wood. Some are built for speed and others for cruising. You will be learning more about the choice of a boat for yourself in the process of becoming sea-worthy; meanwhile, the steps outlined above will help you "get your rudder wet." KERRY THORNLEY

Chapter 2: Large Boats

"I glance at the chronometer...I stare at the thin red lines...if only the shore world were regulated by a force as logical—as honest—as the Law of Storms." STERLING HAYDEN (1)

LARGE BOATS

A former political activist who decided to eliminate the middleman in his crusade for individual freedom, Bill Beer illustrates in the flesh the Permanent Floating Voluntary Society concept. The Beers-Bill, his wife, Sue, and their 3 ½ year-old daughter, Barrie—perform the combination host-crew-guide services of the new family occupation, charter sailing, aboard the TRUE LOVE (which starred as a major prop in the movie, "High Society") about half their days on the Caribbean. When they are not chartering or sailing on a busman's holiday, their boat is tied to the dock in Charlotte Amalie of the U.S. Virgin Islands. Here the Beers make repairs and mingle with the 20 or so other couples in the Virgin Island charter fleet.

The Beers acquired the capital necessary for setting up their new business by selling all their property "down to the TV set." Then they traveled to Connecticut where they purchased the TRUE LOVE.

At this time Sue Beer had no sailing experience and Bill had never owned a boat. They learned seamanship the hard way – under the tutorage of a dense fog, a churning inlet, a sandbar, 200 miles of inlet waterway, and a storm in the Atlantic, in that order, on the trip down to the Caribbean – which prepared them for successful sail navigation of the reef-strewn, poorly-charted Bahamas archipelago when their motor blew up near the end of the voyage.

But now Bill can say, "We have a freedom and an independence matched by few and the solid security of near self-sufficiency. We could ask no more." (2)

Charter sailing tourists in colorful parts of the world, as the Beers are doing, is a good way to make money while living at sea, but it is not the only way in which a large boat can serve as a tool of production. Simple freedom from police harassment for group activities – such as wild parties, clandestine political meetings, illegal medical operations – is a valuable condition which a boat captain can provide for a fee. In addition, he can run cargoes to out-of-the-way places unserviced by major shippers, provide transportation to escaping political refugees, and undertake speculative anti-State ventures – such as the smuggling of American cigarettes into Spain, where high tariffs make such operations, however dangerous, extremely profitable. Smuggling opportunities in a world of antilibertarian trade policies, in fact, are legion – one can take diamonds out of Africa and South America, run arms to rebels in Cuba, land used auto and refrigerator parts in Mexico, bring gold into certain near-totalitarian countries where ownership of some is unlawful...all for life, liberty, and property.

Large boats, in short, offer a way to liberty for those interested in economic as well as personal freedom but who yet do no possess capital necessary for such Permanent Floating Voluntary ventures as shipping lines or man-made islands, to be discussed in the future articles of this series. KERRY THORNLEY

(1) WANDERER by Sterling Hayden (Knopf, 1963)
(2) "A New Life at Sea For Family" by Bill Beer in the Santa Monica EVENING OUTLOOK (WEST Magazine Section) of 16 July, 1966.

Chapter 3: Ships And Shipping

"The term 'cheap flags' refers to the three States, Panama, Liberia, and Honduras, which lend their flag indiscriminately to all ships provided the owners pay once a registration fee and a very low yearly registration tax. Apart from this the shipowners sailing under the 'cheap flag' are not subject to taxation...Furthermore, this freedom from taxes is guaranteed by the law at the same low level in Liberia for 20 and in Honduras for 30 years. It is most interesting that thus three small and underdeveloped States achieved foremost positions in the world shipping market in spite of the various obstructionist efforts by others, States and competitors..." –PEACE PLANS (1)

SHIPS AND SHIPPING

During the last century no voice was louder in calling for government intervention than that of the American shipping industry. Not only did the shippers want subsidies (in order to better compete with the subsidized lines of England), but they were quite willing to tolerate – and sometimes even encourage – trade tariffs as a means of enticing Congress to grant them privileged status. They got their intervention. Now American shipping is on an overall decline – and shippers are demanding increased subsidies (in order to better compete with the nonsubsidized "cheap flag" lines)! If it has seriously occurred to any American shipowner that the industry's trouble is due to the "expensive flag" of tariffs, make-work legal regulations and, yes, subsidies (for other people) and the resulting taxation – he is probably no long owner of an American (registration-wise) ship. For the most cheerful thing an American shipper can hope for besides a handout, these days, is a good and bloody full-scale war.

Keeping this in mind along with the corollary that anyone in close sympathy with the policies of American shippers cannot be expected to have much understanding of economics, the interested libertarian will find THE PRINCIPLES OF OCEAN TRANSPORTATION by James Vernon Metcalfe (a Professor of Foreign Trade at Seattle University) a very fine book. Chief among its virtues is its comprehensive yet relatively concise approach to a field that is usually written about in either a highly specialized manner or in a style so popular as to be superficial. THE PRINCIPLES OF OCEAN TRANSPORTATION is the introductory book for the libertarian interested in taking advantage of the Freedom of the High Seas on a heavy-industry level. It provides orientation in all aspects of operating merchant vessels.

The chapter titles are: Ship Characteristics; Ship and Cargo Measurements; Before the Vessel Arrives; Entering a Vessel From a Foreign Port; Terminal Operation; Vessel in Port; Cargo Handling; Cargo Procurement; Cargo Stowage; Vessel Stability; Cargo Documentation; Ocean Freight Rates; Vessel at Sea; Vessel Chartering; Foreign Freight Forwarders; Marine Insurance; Admiralty and Maritime Law; Labor Relations; Ocean Shipping via Canals; World Fleets and Ports; Domestic Commerce of the United States; The United States Merchant Marine; and Reports from the Lookouts. This book can be purchased from the publishers, Simmons-Boardman Books (30 Church St., New York 10007, 1959), for $5.50.

The prime consideration with regard to merchant shipping is capital. Unless you have or can raise several hundred thousand dollars, starting a shipping line is out of the question. (2) Possibly a number of libertarian businessmen will form a company for precisely this reason – for no industry is less physically subject to State harassment, and therefore any better prospect for long-term investment, than ocean transportation.

Another possibility is for associations of libertarians to form, each for the purpose of buying one ship, and for these associations to cooperate under a single company trade mark. Each association could represent a particular faction within the movement. Thus one might envision a ship with a limited constitutional government all of its own sailing beside one without any government at all. And perhaps there would be an aircraft carrier called the HENRY GEORGE upon which the captain collected "deck rents," while the sailors aboard the schooner GREEN REVOLUTION experimented with farming at sea. The possibilities for cooperation and diversity are at least intriguing. And the Kerista people will be pleased to know that ships under at least two present-day flags have both male and female crew members.

Finally, should the day ever come that Agoric Shipping Lines (or whatever) would decide to be done altogether with the political powers of the world, many existing merchant ships (including all those built with U.S. subsidy money) are specially made for quick conversion to fighting status, so it would not be the usual matter of armed government goons saying to unarmed businessmen, "Come let us reason together." KERRY THORNLEY

(1) PEACE PLANS (J. M. Zube, Wilshire St., Berrima, N. S. W., Australia), issue no. 7, page 25. This quote translated by Zube from a review in HEFT (a German publication) by Solneman. It appears in full as part of a two-and-a-half page proposal in PEACE PLANS entitled "Freedom of the High Seas to be Extended to Continents," an excellent article in its own right.

(2) Now and again one hears of "war surplus liberty ships" or something of that order for sale at less than a hundred-thousand dollars. By the time such vessels were put into sailing order, I have it on good authority, a fantastic monetary outlay would be needed. I have not priced ships extensively but do know of one medium-sized tanker in bad condition that was valued at $400,000. Of new ships, those made in Japan are said to be among the most reasonable and those built in the United State are exorbitant at no appreciable increase in quality.

Chapter 4: Marine Cities

"In Japan a restaurant has been planned under the ocean where patrons can watch the fish and vice-versa. And perhaps it won't be long before some enterprising American builds a resort hotel nestled twelve fathoms down on the pure white sand of a reef valley and hemmed in on all sides by tumbling gardens of coral and the constantly changing, multicolored life of the sea." – THE BOUNTIFUL SEA (1)

MARINE CITIES
Many previous issues of INNOVATOR have contained reports on the "pirate" industries of the North Sea – commercial endeavors which do not pay "protection" money to the governments of Europe, since they are located outside the territorial boundaries of some, as defined by International Law. As the food, mineral, and living space potential of the sea come more under the control of technology, enterprises of this nature increase in number on continental shelf areas all over the world.

Farming the sea, for both fish and edible sea-weed, is emerging from the experimental stage. Some twenty percent of Japan's coal is mined from beneath the ocean floor, and countless other pilot mining projects – for every mineral imaginable – are under way around the globe. The bottom of the sea is also already a widely recognized storage place. One U.S. city stores its water supply beneath its harbor and fuel has been stored successfully by the U.S. Navy in the Gulf of Mexico. The prospect of sea cities, on and under the surface, is now taken for granted by informed prognosticators – and the prospect is immediate.

There are two ways libertarians can take advantage of these developments:

(1) FOCUS EDUCATIONAL EFFORTS on the men and women who are involved in these projects. Meet and become acquainted with ocean frontiersmen. (Think how handy such friends might be in an economic or political crisis!) Ask them many questions. Find out what their professional problems are and suggest solutions that are in accord with their libertarian principles. Inform them of their rights above the law. Tell them how to foil the statist mentality and defeat the expansionist efforts of the national bureaucracies. (These are

things you can do no matter where you live. The marine biology professor at a Midwest College is as much a part of what is virtually a Second Industrial Revolution as the hypothetical "enterprising American" who builds a resort twelve fathoms down. And if you live in an Arizona ghost town you can still write letters, or even newspaper columns.) Demonstrate to the marine pioneer that his prime advantage is the long tradition of Freedom of the High Seas, and that it will be personally profitable to him if he does all that is within his power to maintain it.

(2) CONCENTRATE INVESTMENT OF RESOURCES on maritime metropolis projects, particularly on man-made floating islands and other highly mobile capital, since this can best be defended against future attempts at control or confiscation by the world powers. (Another possibility that should not be entirely ignored though, is the "bubble on the bottom" concept, especially as a means of hiding large quantities of property. Construction costs are often less, and protection from storms is usually superior.) Nor are monetary resources all that can be invested. A student entering the university can direct his studies toward aspects of the oceanic scene, in most cases with little or no shift in his field of interest. The student of law, for example, can specialize in Maritime and International Law. The engineer can focus on marine engineering, etc. Servicing and communications industries will also have a market in marine communities. A private sea-air postal system and a few libertarian-edited marine industrial journals might get things off to a good start.

Future articles in this series will report on specific commercial activities which are now thriving in salt water, many of which are probably on the sites of the free cities of tomorrow's voluntary world.
KERRY THORNLEY.

(1) THE BOUNTIFUL SEA by Seabrook Hull (Prentice-Hall, 1964).

Chapter 5: Aquaculture

"Control of foodstuffs in the sea has a beginning similar to that of its counterpart of land. Start with the weeds. When the weeds become cultured, we call them plants. Once culture takes hold, then yield accelerates, and we have more than enough for our immediate needs."
-ROBERT M. SNYDER (1)

AQUACULTURE

Japan is the world's leading nation when it comes to farming the sea. Over twenty kinds of seaplant, for example, are marketed there for eating purposes. Some of these are harvested wild, but many are cultivated from seed, transplanted to oceanic nets, and harvested about two months later. They are then dried on sheets on bamboo mats. This end product, while is usually requires of the Occidental that he develop a taste for it, is rich in vitamins, and very popular with the natives of Japan.

In 1954 a Dr. Matosaku opened the first commercial shrimp farms in Japan. Nine years later he was shipping seventy pounds of shrimp per day. He has bred shrimp up to eight inches in length. And he is also breeding prawns – a total of 2,860 pounds in 1961, 500 tons in 1962, and more than 1,000 tons in 1963.

Another popular Oriental food is a shellfish called the wreath shell. These have been artificially inseminated and a single batch of 200,000 eggs produced per insemination.

The Japanese also suspend racks from floats and grow oysters upon them in quantities of about 20,000 tons per year. And about 2,200 tons of eels are harvested each year on over 750 eel farms. In addition bream, blowfish, bass, halibut, and grey mullet are also bred by "fish ranchers." And when the market is bad, there are fatteners who will buy part of a fish crop to retain in holding tanks for speculative purposes.

The market is open for the ambitious entrepreneur who is ready to stake out his claim and start farming somewhere beyond the three-mile-long arms of the landgoing pirates of our time. KERRY THORNLEY

(1) From the foreword of Seabrook Hull's THE BOUNTIFUL SEA (Prentice-Hall, 1964). The statistics on Japanese aquaculture are also from this book.

Chapter 6: Marine Mining

"Undersea mining in some areas is already big business...Magnesium is extracted directly from seawater. Oil and sulfur have been taken from beneath the sea floor for many years. The ocean is already being opened up for commerce, and before long private industry will be spending more on undersea commerce than Government now spends on undersea warfare." (1)

MARINE MINING

Da Beers Consolidated Mines, Ltd. is engaged in undersea diamond prospecting and mining off the coast of South Africa. Global Marine Exploration Company searches for undersea oil in deep water. Marine Diamond Company, Ltd. (managed by Texan, S. V. Collins) mines by suction for gems. Ocean Science & Engineering, Inc. designs and builds undersea exploration equipment. Richfield Oil Company and Shell Oil Company are building undersea oil fields. Tideweater Oil Company is engaged in undersea diamond mining. And Yawata Iron and Steel Company of Japan mines iron-bearing sand from the ocean floor.

Other companies are playing less direct roles in mineral exploration of the sea. U.S. Rubber has built and tested undersea storage tanks. Dr. Edwin Link, President of the Link Division of General Precision, Inc. has "camped out" in a pressurized tent on the ocean floor, General Dynamics Corporation is one of the many companies that has conducted studies on undersea transportation. Hughes Aircraft has built submarine robot units to assist in the installation of oil wells.

To list all the minerals that are or will be mined from the ocean would simply be an exercise in recitation of the names of most of the elements. A similar exercise would be to attempt a complete list of the companies involved in one manner or another in ocean mining. The important thing to realize is that the heaviest industry is being drawn into this Second Industrial Revolution in the search for minerals. It is therefore essential that libertarians interested in advancing the concept of a Permanent Floating Voluntary Society do some hard thinking with regard to the ever-present problems of property in natural resources.

The First Claim Theory, for example, as some prominent libertarians espouse it (2), would put most future marine mineral exploitation under the control of an aspiring monarchy which calls itself Aqualandia. For his Majesty King Marion I, in a proclamation dated 10 August 1961, published a claim to "all the lands of the world that exist beneath the oceans and other salt water bodies of the world, except that portion of ocean bottom or other salt water bottom lands which are now claimed as the property of the various government in the world, and where such claim is, as of this date recognized as valid by "International Law." The proclamation goes on to assure that "Aqualandia "does not claim any right to govern, regulate or interfere with the present or future use of the waters above its land," and adds that Aqualandia's is patterned after that of England. This proclamation was published in a pamphlet called "The Aqualandian" (The Aqualandia Society, 6812 Santa Monica Blvd., Los Angeles, Calif., 90038) in July of 1966. But somehow I fail to see, speaking only for myself, how recognition of this First Claim (if, indeed, it is the first) would possibly be in my interest.

On the other hand, the standard argument of the most ardent admirers of Henry George, which hold that natural resources should not be claimed by individuals or companies or societies at all, but should be "owned in common" in, at best, a sort of universal profit-sharing plan – and which would tend to condemn the present companies involved in ocean mining for coercively monopolizing the mineral deposits – while certainly more rational than the unmodified First Claim Theory, brings up a host of new problems in its place. And putting aside those which fall into the "who-would-administrate" category entirely, this approach would, unless liberalized, go counter to our primary purpose of winning over to the libertarian position those basic industries now mining the sea.

One factor which may bring about a resolution, at least with regard to the ocean, is the technical difficulties involved. By the time one has extracted minerals of almost any sort from the sea a great deal of thought and energy has been applied. It is far more difficult than driving a claim post into the ground or panning gold. Arbitrary First Claims on behalf of Southern California groups and their like will tend to be ignored, and will be next-to-impossible to enforce. And the Georgists, if they can point out to the mining companies a self-interested motive for voluntarily paying out mineral rent fees to the population at large, will find little opposition from laissez-faire libertarians. In the meantime, it is important that the rest of us develop a rational and simple procedure for establishing ownership of the natural resources in the sea, perhaps along the lines of John Locke's "mixing labor" formula. KERRY THORNLEY

(1) THE BOUNTIFUL SEA by Seabrook Hull (Prentice-Hall, 1964).
(2) See for example, J. Dohn Lewis, THE LAND QUESTION, and Butler Shaffer, PERSONAL DECLARATION OF PRINCIPLES, in the Jan., 1965, and Sept., 1966 issues of INNOVATOR.
(Transcriber's Note: This concludes the 6 part series The *Permanent Floating Voluntary Society* which was originally published in *Innovator*, July to Dec 1966.)

Additional Resources

- **The Vonu Podcast**: If you want to learn more about anything covered in this book, I'd highly recommend you check out the podcast Kyle Rearden and I do. In season 1, we covered the philosophy of vonu, season 2 was the practice of vonu, and the current season, 3, is where we develop and update vonu to the modern day.
    - www.vonupodcast.com
- **Vonu: The Search for Personal Freedom, Number 2 – Letters from Rayo**
    - www.vonupodcast.com/vonu2
- **Vonulife, March 1973 (Special Edition)**
    - www.vonupodcast.com/vl
- **Ocean Freedom Notes**
    - www.vonupodcast.com/ofn
- **Self-Liberation Notes**
    - www.vonupodcast.com/sln
- **Going Mobile**
    - www.vonupodcast.com/gm
- **Low-Cost Living**
    - www.vonupodcast.com/lcl
- **Dwelling Portably [sic]**
    - www.vonupodcast.com/dp
- **Articles About Vonu**
    - www.vonupodcast.com/vonuarticles
- **Liberty Under Attack**: If you're seeking out paths to personal freedom, then you need to check out The Freedom Umbrella of Direct Action and the Direct Action Series.
    - www.libertyunderattack.com/FUDA
    - www.libertyunderattack.com/DAS

- **The Last Bastille Blog**: This is Kyle's blog and it's chockful of incredible, highly valuable information. He has written over 150 book reviews, a couple books pertinent to vonu, and much more.
    - www.thelastbastille.com
- **YouTube**: If you're pursuing any of the lifestyle changes or strategies I covered above, then YouTube will be your best friend. Recommended search terms: "van dwelling," "living aboard a boat," "minimalist sailboating," etc.

OTHER RECOMMENDED BOOKS ON VONU:

THE LIFE OF TOM MARSHALL CHRONICLES THE KNOWN LIFE OF TOM MARSHALL ("RAYO"), THE FOUNDER AND MAIN PROPONENT OF THE FREEDOM STRATEGY, VONU.

#AGORA IS THE "FICTIONAL" STORY OF DANIEL LARUSSO'S JOURNEY INTO THE CRYPTO-ANARCHIST, CYPHERPUNK UNDERGROUND. BASED OFF OF A REAL SECOND REALM COMMUNITY IN BERLIN, LEARN HOW FREEDOM CAN BE BUILT IN THE HERE AND NOW.

VONU: THE SEARCH FOR PERSONAL FREEDOM IS THE BOOK THAT STARTED IT ALL. PUT TOGETHER BY JIM STUMM, THIS COLLECTION OF ARTICLES BY RAYO INTRODUCES THE STRATEGY/PHILOSOHPY OF VONU AND GIVES YOU A LOOK INTO RAYO'S RADICAL LIFESTYLES.

VONU, BOOK 2: LETTERS FROM RAYO IS ANOTHER COLLECTION PUT TOGETHER BY JIM STUMM. HEREIN, YOU'LL READ MANY LETTERS FROM RAYO, GET UPDATES ON THEIR VONU LIFESTYLES, AND MUCH MORE.

If you enjoyed the book and found it valuable, please consider making a one-time bitcoin donation!

Bitcoin: 15Bdzduwt92jYFGFaK2NSkPYFTaLbtonJg

Looking for a liberty-oriented publisher?
We can help!

- Proofreading/Editing
- Kindle/Paperback Formatting
- Audiobook Production/Narration
- Marketing/Promotion
- Illustrations/Graphic Design

WWW.LIBERTYUNDERATTACK.COM/PUBLISH

Printed in Great Britain
by Amazon